WALKS
IN
BRONTË COUNTRY

HILLSIDE GUIDES

LONG DISTANCE WALKS
1• THE WESTMORLAND WAY
2• THE FURNESS WAY
3• THE CUMBERLAND WAY
7• CLEVELAND WAY COMPANION
9• THE NORTH BOWLAND TRAVERSE
(by David Johnson)
16• DALES WAY COMPANION
22• THE COAST TO COAST WALK

CIRCULAR WALKS - YORKSHIRE DALES
4• WALKS IN WHARFEDALE
5• WALKS IN NIDDERDALE
6• WALKS IN THE CRAVEN DALES
8• WALKS IN WENSLEYDALE
10• WALKS IN THREE PEAKS COUNTRY
11• WALKS IN SWALEDALE
20• RAMBLES IN WHARFEDALE
21• WALKS ON THE HOWGILL FELLS

CIRCULAR WALKS - NORTH YORK MOORS
13• WESTERN - Cleveland/Hambleton Hills
14• SOUTHERN - Rosedale/Farndale/Bransdale
15• NORTHERN - Eskdale and the Coast

CIRCULAR WALKS - SOUTH PENNINES
12• WALKS IN BRONTE COUNTRY
17• WALKS IN CALDERDALE

HILLWALKING - LAKE DISTRICT
18• OVER LAKELAND MOUNTAINS
19• OVER LAKELAND FELLS

FREEDOM OF THE DALES
40 selected walks
Full colour hardback

---

80 DALES WALKS
Omnibus edition of Books 4,6,8,11 and (in part)10,21
Published by Cordee, Leicester

WALKS
IN
BRONTË COUNTRY

by

Paul Hannon

HILLSIDE  PUBLICATIONS

HILLSIDE PUBLICATIONS
11 Nessfield Grove
Exley Head
Keighley
West Yorkshire
BD22 6NU

First published 1987
3rd (Revised) impression 1993

TO
Acton, Currer and Ellis Bell

Page 1 : Boulsworth summit, looking to Pendle Hill
(Walk 11)
Page 7: sign hanging outside Brontë Parsonage
(Walks 1 and 7)

The maps in this book are based upon
the 1909 – 1934 Ordnance Survey 1:10,560 maps

ISBN   1 870141 21 0

Printed in Great Britain by
Carnmor Print and Design
95/97 London Road
Preston
Lancashire
PR1 4BA

INTRODUCTION

'South Pennines' is the generally accepted term for describing that part of the Pennine range lying between the Yorkshire Dales and the Peak District, and the area explored in these pages is the northernmost section commencing at the Aire Gap at Skipton and halting at the watershed with Calderdale. The western and eastern boundaries are clearly defined by the roads from Skipton to Colne and Bingley respectively, the latter following the deep trough of the Aire Valley.

Though not the geographical centre of the area, Haworth is certainly the major focal point, made internationally famous by the Brontë sisters, who themselves played a part in promoting the neighbouring moorland. Haworth looks over the Worth Valley, which, aided by its steam railway, drives a wedge into the heart of the high moors which dominate this broader southern portion of the area. Reservoirs and gritstone outcrops occur with regularity hereabouts, but soon fade away in the northern section around Lothersdale and South Craven, where the moorland itself makes only isolated appearances. Though of modest proportions, our area embraces no less than three counties, with half of the walks in West Yorkshire and the remainder divided between North Yorkshire and Lancashire.

The district is liberally scattered with villages, almost all of which are dominated by their 'dark satanic mills', a reminder that this is the fringe of the industrial West Riding. More recently these villages have grown to accommodate people working in the towns around the perimeter. Within the area the more traditional industry of quarrying was clearly once quite extensive, though rarely on any large scale. Lead mining also made a modest contribution near Skipton.

The various facilities to be found at places on the walks are listed on page 8, giving a general idea of what to expect. Bus services in the area are, by today's standards, very good, although they deteriorate north of the Cross Hills-Colne road. The four bordering towns of Skipton, Keighley, Bingley and Colne all have railway stations, as have the villages of Cononley and Steeton/Silsden between Keighley and Skipton. The Worth Valley Railway leaves the main line at Keighley, with further stations at Ingrow West, Damems, Oakworth, Haworth and Oxenhope. The entry 'car park' is to show public parking areas, although most of the public houses also have car parks that might be taken advantage of if considering patronising the said establishment!

The 18 walks described range in length from 4 to 8 miles, and all are circular. An average distance of 5½ miles makes them ideal for half-day rambles. Each walk has its own chapter comprising of 'immediate impression' diagram, detailed narrative and strip map, and notes and illustrations of features of interest.

Although the strip-maps illustrating each walk will safely guide one around, they are unable to show features of the surrounding countryside. Recommended are Ordnance Survey maps:

1:50,000   Landranger sheets 103 and 104

1:25,000   Pathfinder sheets 670, 671, 681, 682
Use of Outdoor Leisure sheet 21 - South Pennines makes sheet 681 unnecessary, and leaves 671 covering only Walk 4, and 682 only Walks 10 and 14.

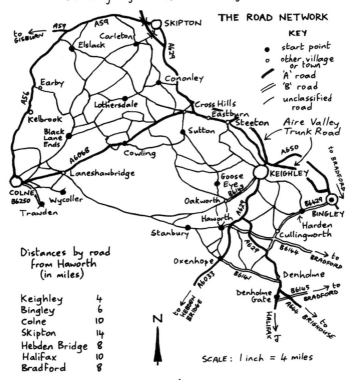

THE ROAD NETWORK

KEY

● start point
○ other village or town
╱ 'A' road
╱╱ 'B' road
╱ unclassified road

Distances by road
from Haworth
(in miles)

Keighley	4
Bingley	6
Colne	10
Skipton	14
Hebden Bridge	8
Halifax	10
Bradford	8

N

SCALE: 1 inch = 4 miles

6

THE BRONTËS OF HAWORTH

No guide to this district, not even a book of walks, could leave out a brief introduction to the Family who put this corner of Yorkshire Firmly on the map.

     The Brontës came to Haworth in 1820 to live in the Parsonage where all but one of them were to end their lives. The father, the Rev. Patrick Brontë, had taken the curacy here after a spell at Thornton near Bradford: he was born in Ireland while his wife Maria hailed from Cornwall. Within five years she and the eldest daughters Maria and Elizabeth had passed on, leaving the Four other children to reach adulthood.

     The three sisters departed on numerous occasions to spend largely unsuccessful spells as governesses in other parts of the county, while Branwell, the only brother, showed promise as an artist. His progress, however, soon halted, and after a spell as a railway clerk he returned home: stricken by illness he saw out his closing years as a regular of the Black Bull, adjacent to the church.

     Meanwhile the sisters had also returned to the fold, but in their cases to begin their successful literary careers. When the first novels were published Emily and Anne had little time to enjoy any acclaim, for their deaths rapidly followed the demise of Branwell in 1848. Anne was buried in Scarborough, her works a little overshadowed by Emily's masterpiece *Wuthering Heights*. Charlotte's first published novel *Jane Eyre* was followed by further works. She even survived long enough to marry the Rev. Nicholls in 1854, though tragically her flame was also to burn out the very next year. Thus Patrick Brontë was to outlive all his children, attaining the ripe old age of 84. The ldest, Charlotte, had not even reached middle age.

     What makes the story of the Brontë sisters so memorable is the nature of the background to their literary achievements, notably the intense hardship and adversity the family had faced, and more appreciably still the brooding mass of moorland beyond their home, where they sought and found untold inspiration.

FACILITIES ON THE WALKS

	Accommodation	Inn	Car Park	Bus service	Post Office	Shop	WC	Payphone
Bingley	✓	✓	✓	✓	✓	✓	✓	✓
Black Lane Ends		✓						
Carleton		✓		✓	✓	✓		✓
Cononley		✓	✓	✓	✓	✓	✓	✓
Cowling	✓	✓		✓	✓	✓	✓	✓
Denholme		✓		✓	✓	✓	✓	✓
Denholme Gate	✓	✓		✓				
Eastburn		✓		✓	✓			✓
Elslack		✓						✓
Goose Eye		✓		✓				✓
Harden		✓		✓	✓	✓	✓	✓
Haworth	✓	✓	✓	✓	✓	✓	✓	✓
Leeming	✓	✓		✓				✓
Lothersdale	✓	✓			✓			✓
Oxenhope	✓	✓	✓	✓	✓	✓	✓	✓
St. Ives			✓	✓			✓	
Stanbury	✓	✓		✓	✓			✓
Sutton		✓		✓	✓	✓	✓	✓
Trawden		✓		✓	✓	✓	✓	✓
Wycoller			✓			✓		

There are youth hostels at Haworth and Earby

SOME USEFUL ADDRESSES

Ramblers' Association
1/5 Wandsworth Road, London SW8 2XX
Tel. 071- 582 6878

Youth Hostels Association
Trevelyan House, St. Albans, Herts. AL1 2DY
Tel. 0727 - 55215

Yorkshire and Humberside Tourist Board
312 Tadcaster Road, York YO2 2HF
Tel. 0904 - 707961

North West Tourist Board
The Last Drop Village, Bromley Cross, Bolton, Lancs. BL7 9PZ
Tel. 0204 - 591511

Tourist Information – Haworth
2 West Lane, Haworth, Keighley BD22 8EF
Tel. 0535 - 642329

Tourist Information – Skipton
Victoria Square, Skipton, North Yorkshire
Tel. 0756 - 792809

Keighley and District Travel Ltd
Bus Station, Townfieldgate, Keighley
Tel. 0535 - 603284
also at Keighley Rd, Skipton (0756 - 795331)

Burnley and Pendle Transport
Queensgate Depot, Colne Rd, Burnley, Lancs. BB10 1HH
Tel. 0282 - 25244

Brontë Parsonage Museum
Church Street, Haworth, Keighley BD22 8DR
Tel. 0535-642323

Keighley and Worth Valley Railway
Haworth Station, Haworth, Keighley BD22 8NJ
Tel. 0535-645214

THE WALKS

Listed below are the 18 walks described, the walk number being the key to easy location in the guide

WALK	TITLE	MILES
1	THE WORTH VALLEY	5
2	PINHAW BEACON	$6\frac{1}{4}$
3	THORNTON MOOR AND DOE PARK	$5\frac{1}{2}$
4	SUTTON CLOUGH AND EASTBURN CRAG	$4\frac{3}{4}$
5	BENEATH OXENHOPE MOOR	$5\frac{1}{4}$
6	THE MONUMENTS OF EARL CRAG	$6\frac{1}{4}$
7	TOP WITHINS AND HAWORTH MOOR	8
8	GREAT EDGE AND KELBROOK MOOR	$4\frac{3}{4}$
9	THE PONDEN AREA	4
10	GOIT STOCK WOOD AND HARDEN MOOR	6
11	BOULSWORTH HILL	5
12	AROUND THE GIB	$4\frac{1}{4}$
13	BROW MOOR AND BRIDGEHOUSE BECK	$4\frac{3}{4}$
14	ST. IVES AND DRUID'S ALTAR	$5\frac{3}{4}$
15	TOW TOP AND COWLING HILL	4
16	WYCOLLER COUNTRY PARK	$4\frac{1}{2}$
17	KEIGHLEY MOOR AND NEWSHOLME DEAN	7
18	CARLETON GLEN AND RAMSHAW	$4\frac{1}{2}$

THE WALKS

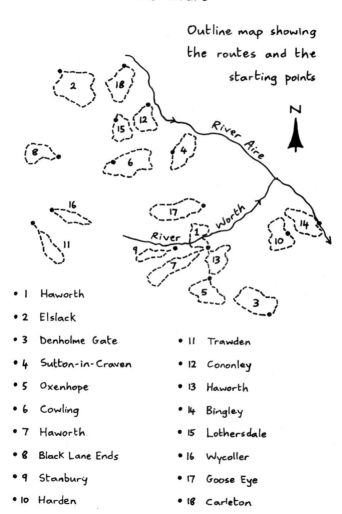

Outline map showing the routes and the starting points

N

- 1 Haworth
- 2 Elslack
- 3 Denholme Gate
- 4 Sutton-in-Craven
- 5 Oxenhope
- 6 Cowling
- 7 Haworth
- 8 Black Lane Ends
- 9 Stanbury
- 10 Harden
- 11 Trawden
- 12 Cononley
- 13 Haworth
- 14 Bingley
- 15 Lothersdale
- 16 Wycoller
- 17 Goose Eye
- 18 Carleton

WALK 1

5 miles

| THE WORTH VALLEY |

from Haworth

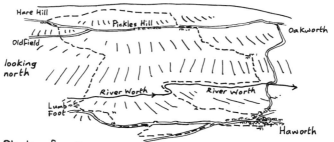

Plenty of ups and downs in this exploration of the lesser known parts of the Worth Valley

Park in one of Haworth's car parks, preferably the Museum car park at the top of the Main Street

| THE WALK |

From the church take the short, cobbled road up to the Parsonage Museum, just beyond which it becomes a footpath, emerging to cross a field to join West Lane at a wicket gate. Go left and then left again up Cemetery Road onto the moorland slopes of Penistone Hill. On reaching the cemetery fork right down a broad green track: at a gate turn sharp right, leaving the track to follow a wall down onto a lane.

Turn down it to the bottom of the hill, then go right in front of a row of cottages. Just beyond use a stile on the left to climb a field to Milking Hill Farm. Pass along the front and out via its access road onto a junction. Turn right down the narrow lane to Lumb Foot, continuing down a track between the buildings to an attractive footbridge over the River Worth. A good path immediately climbs along the edge of a wooded gill. At a path junction at the top go left to cross a stile and the tiny beck, then on a broad green way and a field to Street Head Farm. Keep right of the buildings and up the access track onto a lane. Cross straight over to a gate into a field and climb by a wall to join a higher, parallel lane. Turn left to reach the *Grouse* inn.

At this point we leave the road along an enclosed track opposite the hostelry. It is followed to a junction of tracks by a cottage, and straight on a little further down the gradually declining Turnshaw Road (still a rough track). Leave it at the first building (a renovated farmhouse) on the right, dropping down through stiles on its left side to follow its drive out onto a road. Go left about 150 yards until the third drive on the right – look for the 'notable' gateposts. Follow it past the house and down to Green Well farm. Keep left of the farm and straight down a green way. Take a stile on the left at the bottom and cross two fields, then drop half-right to a rather good stile. Follow the wall away from it, soon taking a stile in that wall to descend to West Field farm.

On emerging onto its drive cross straight over to a small gate and continue the descent to join another track. Just below it is a stile, and from it the river Worth is accompanied upstream. At the next stile but one the path is transported away from the river until another stile, but many walkers have clearly remained with it almost as far as the latter stile. Here the river is rejoined to lead round to Long Bridge, a shapely stone footbridge.

Cross it and follow the green lane climbing away to reach a house. Go left in front of it, through a tiny snicket and then across a field-top to a stile in the fence opposite. Stay with the right-hand wall to a gate from where a track runs, largely enclosed, to emerge back into Haworth village. Go right and then left to return to the church.

Laverock Hall

Lower Laithe Reservoir, with Stanbury Moor, Ponden Clough and Stanbury, from Hill Top, Penistone Hill Country Park

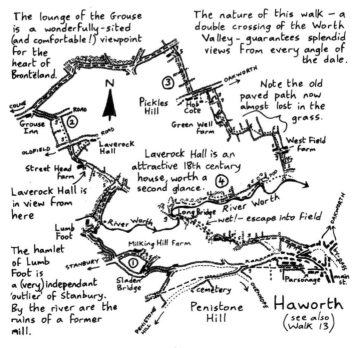

The lounge of the Grouse is a wonderfully-sited (and comfortable!) viewpoint for the heart of Brontëland.

The nature of this walk — a double crossing of the Worth Valley — guarantees splendid views from every angle of the dale.

Note the old paved path now almost lost in the grass.

Laverock Hall is an attractive 18th century house, worth a second glance.

Laverock Hall is in view from here

The hamlet of Lumb Foot is a (very) independant 'outlier' of Stanbury. By the river are the ruins of a former mill.

COLNE
ROAD
Grouse Inn
②
ROAD
OLDFIELD
Laverock Hall
Street Head Farm
N
③
Pickles Hill
Hob Cote
OAKWORTH
Green Well Farm
West Field Farm
④
River Worth
Long Bridge
wet! — escape into field
River Worth
Lumb Foot
Milking Hill Farm
STANBURY
①
Slader Bridge
cemetery
Penistone Hill
PENISTONE HILL
OXENHOPE
Parsonage
OAKWORTH
LEES LANE
main st.
Haworth
(see also)
(Walk 13)

WALK 2
6¼ miles

from Elslack

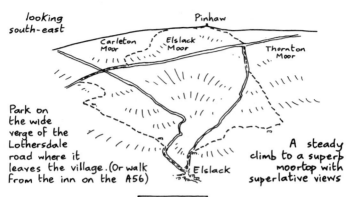

looking south-east

Pinhaw

Carleton Moor

Elslack Moor

Thornton Moor

Park on the wide verge of the Lothersdale road where it leaves the village. (Or walk from the inn on the A56)

Elslack

A steady climb to a superb moortop with superlative views

THE WALK

From the village centre take the Lothersdale road (Moor Lane), and at the first opportunity leave by a track left to Smearber Farm. On entering the yard go through the gate across and follow the wall away. When it parts company continue on to a stile in the next wall. The route now maintains a near-straight course through numerous fields, each time with a well placed stile. When finally there is no stile ahead take a gate on the right onto open moorland.

A path now follows the left-hand wall to a gate in it past a plantation. Cross the field to a cattle-grid and accompany a farm road up towards Lower Scarcliff, going left of it and over two more cattle-grids. Here leave the track by a lesser track right, by a wall behind the farm. This track ends at the uninhabited Higher Scarcliff. Now rise gently left across the moor around the slope to the left. A sunken path can be traced, but after levelling out it falters. Keep left of some grouse-butts to join up with a wall which runs down to a road.

Head right up to a crossroads, keeping straight on to a cattle-grid. Leave the road by a stile in the left-hand wall and hug the departing wall up onto Carleton Moor. A generally clear path accompanies it over the moor-top and begins a descent to Lothersdale. Eventually an intervening wall is met: from the stile

15

go right to another stile a few yards along. The Pennine Way is now joined, and immediately leads back onto Elslack Moor. A clear path now rises over the moor to the Ordnance column atop Pinhaw Beacon. After a suitable break continue down to meet a wall before arriving at a road junction, crossing straight over and down the lane opposite.

At a track forking left we remain on the Pennine Way, going through a stile and descending a rough moor by a wall. Eventually a stile is met, and a little below a rather novel footbridge crosses both beck and wall. Here we leave the Pennine Way and aim straight across the field to a gate immediately above the farm buildings of Wood House.

Follow its access track to the right, and half-way along the field take a stile in the wall to bear half-right to the next stile. From it accompany the left-hand wall on a gradual descent. After two more stiles leave the wall at a short row of trees, and aim half-right for a farm. At the bottom of the hill is a gate in a fence, and across a narrow pasture a stile by a gate admits onto a lane just above the farm. Elslack is now but a couple of minutes down the lane.

Elslack

N

* The left-hand track from the gate leads down to the youth hostel at Earby, a regular target for Pennine Wayfarers.

Wood House (farm)

ELSLACK

⑥

⑤

Pinhaw Beacon, looking to Pendle Hill

Elslack is a tiny community hidden just off the Skipton–Colne road. The village 'centre' consists of a grouping of dignified dwellings around a miniscule green. The inn near the main road bears the arms of the big local family of nearby Broughton Hall.

Here at Elslack the Romans had a fort on their road from Ribchester to Ilkley.

Despite its modest altitude Pinhaw is the highest point north of the Cross Hills–Colne road until the Yorkshire Dales north of Skipton. As a result it boasts an extensive 360° panorama, with those Dales Fells the best features. Without its more modern adornments the summit remains highly distinguishable as the raised site of a beacon (can you pick out Malham Cove?). The moor on which it stands is adorned with notices advising of its private ownership by the Elslack Estate Co.

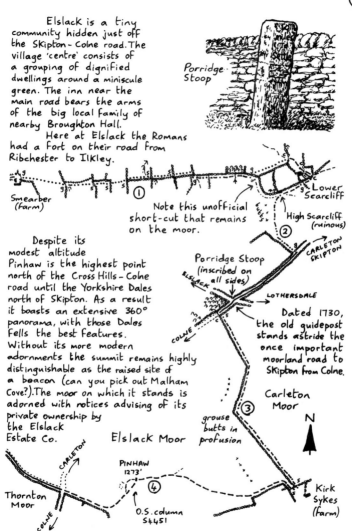

Porridge Stoop

Smearber (farm)

① Note this unofficial short-cut that remains on the moor.

Lower Scarcliff

High Scarcliff (ruinous)

CARLETON SKIPTON

Porridge Stoop (inscribed on all sides)

ELSLACK

COLNE

LOTHERSDALE

②

Dated 1730, the old guidepost stands astride the once important moorland road to Skipton from Colne.

Carleton Moor

N

grouse butts in profusion

③

Elslack Moor

CARLETON

PINHAW 1273'

④

Thornton Moor

COLNE

O.S. column 54451

Kirk Sykes (farm)

17

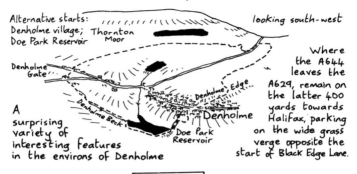

WALK 3
5½ miles

THORNTON MOOR AND DOE PARK
From Denholme Gate

looking south-west

Alternative starts:
Denholme village;
Doe Park Reservoir

Thornton Moor

Denholme Gate

Denholme Edge

Denholme Beck

Denholme

Doe Park Reservoir

A surprising variety of interesting features in the environs of Denholme

Where the A644 leaves the A629, remain on the latter 400 yards towards Halifax, parking on the wide grass verge opposite the start of Black Edge Lane.

THE WALK

The first mile and a half of this walk simply involves following the no-nonsense course of Black Edge Lane (a walled track), which half way along becomes known as Thornton Moor Road. When it becomes surfaced at a reservoir house, ignore a branch right and go a little further to a T-junction. Here take a gate on the right and follow another rough lane until it becomes surfaced at an enthusiastically-pointed cottage. Now go right again up a grassy byway to join a water authority access road, continuing on it to emerge onto a public road.

Turn left past the farm, and as the road begins to drop take a stile on the right. Follow the wall away to another stile, then go right again to accompany a wall through several intervening walls. A walled section is entered until it turns sharp right: here take a gate on the left to follow a splendid green track by a wall. From a stile at the end the wall switches to our left as we pass through several fine stiles. On meeting a green lane take the small gate opposite and follow the wall to the left. At a stile the top of Denholme Edge is gained, and a path heads right by the wall along the top. Beyond the next stile above a housing estate the path drops through heather onto a rough lane to join the main road through Denholme. Go right.

Opposite the *Little Bull* turn down a vague path that is soon channelled between houses, over a suburban road and down another field, to bear right with a fence (above the old railway) onto a road. Turn left down the road, which soon descends to Doe Park Reservoir. Cross the embankment and follow

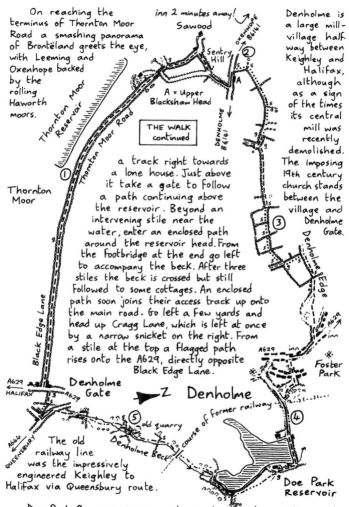

On reaching the terminus of Thornton Moor Road a smashing panorama of Brontëland greets the eye, with Leeming and Oxenhope backed by the rolling Haworth moors.

inn 2 minutes away!
Sawood

Sentry Hill

A = Upper Blackshaw Head

Thornton Moor Reservoir

Thornton Moor Road

Thornton Moor

THE WALK continued

Denholme Beck

OXENHOPE B6141

Denholme is a large mill-village half-way between Keighley and Halifax, although as a sign of the times its central mill was recently demolished. The imposing 19th century church stands between the village and Denholme Gate.

Denholme Edge

A629

inn

Foster Park

a track right towards a lone house. Just above it take a gate to follow a path continuing above the reservoir. Beyond an intervening stile near the water, enter an enclosed path around the reservoir head. From the footbridge at the end go left to accompany the beck. After three stiles the beck is crossed but still followed to some cottages. An enclosed path soon joins their access track up onto the main road. Go left a few yards and head up Cragg Lane, which is left at once by a narrow snicket on the right. From a stile at the top a flagged path rises onto the A629, directly opposite Black Edge Lane.

Black Edge Lane

A629 HALIFAX

Denholme Gate

Denholme

A6141 QUEENSBURY

old quarry

Denholme Beck

course of former railway

The old railway line was the impressively engineered Keighley to Halifax via Queensbury route.

Doe Park Reservoir

Doe Park Reservoir is a popular sailing centre. The path around its head is excellently flagged, and a mini nature-trail.

WALK 4

4¾ miles

from Sutton-in-Craven

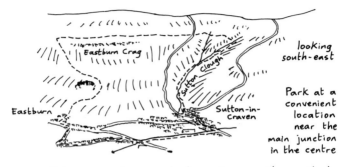

looking south-east

Park at a convenient location near the main junction in the centre

Colourful surroundings and steep slopes, with excellent views of mid-Airedale and well beyond

THE WALK

From the main junction in the village centre (bounded by the park, a mill and the *Black Bull* inn) head along the road signposted to Laycock. Keep left along the High Street and at a fork take the unsigned road straight ahead between these two roads. Guarded by a splendid archway, this is Hall Drive, which soon becomes a rough road. Beyond the houses a footbridge carries us over the beck and a wide track heads into the trees.

Pass an arched, a foot, then a concrete bridge before succumbing to a small footbridge. A good path accompanies the opposite bank, and just above a confluence the climbing begins. The path stays close to the beck up this wooded ravine until it turns to climb steeply right: here cross to the opposite bank where a few yards upstream a path doubles back up the slope to the left. The woods are left at a small gate at the top, then make for the farm up to the right.

A corner stile admits to the left side of the house, and just across is a low stile. From it descend the field to a beck, taking a stile on the left to join a path downstream. Within 50 yards leave it by steps down to cross the beck, with a stile just a little beyond. Across the field-bottom is a grand stile with steps, from where rise through dense shrubbery to find a stile behind. Now climb with the wall on the right to cross two intervening wall-stiles just right of a barn. Turn left along the farm road to emerge via a farm onto a lane.

Cross straight over to Long House, continuing past it on a narrow green lane. At its terminus cross to a gate, and on to a missing stile at the end of the next field. Once over, cross the rough pasture to a stile in the far right corner, and just above is a gate to enter the yard of Valley Farm. Keep straight on through gates to enter a fine green lane which doesn't last long enough. At its demise head straight on to another missing stile in the facing wall, which is probably best negotiated at its right-hand corner.

Remain with the right-hand wall to a gateway with a gate behind: up to the right is Summer House Farm. Follow the left-hand wall to join the farm-road, remaining with it until a bend before it becomes surfaced. Here take a track descending from a gate on the left. A short enclosed section leads to the rim of a quarry: the track drops down beyond it to become enclosed again, entering Eastburn as a paved lane.

The main road is joined by the post office, and a well-sited pedestrian crossing conveys us across. Go left a few yards before escaping down Green Lane, turning left at the bottom onto Lyon Road before rejoining the main road. Go right and when possible cross over, leaving it along a surfaced path immediately after crossing Holme Beck. This path now shadows the beck all the way to the road through Sutton. Turn left to return to the start, neatly avoiding most of the road by concluding in the pleasant surroundings of the public park.

The stocks, Sutton Park

Sutton village centre

Sutton-in-Craven (locally just Sutton, as it's a long way to the next Sutton) is a sizeable village in the shadow of steep hills to the south. It is dominated by its large mills, and its older High Street area with cottages, inns and the public park is altogether attractive.

Earl Crag from Eastburn Bridge

Between Valley Farm and Eastburn Bridge we leave North Yorkshire for West Yorkshire.

KILDWICK A629

works   Lyon Road

Eastburn Bridge

Green Lane

Eastburn

A629 (old road)   inn

PO   STEETON → A629

④

Holme Beck

Moor Lane

CROSS HILLS

mill

Sutton Park

TO A629

③

old quarry

seats in profusion (of more use if walking the route clockwise, i.e in ascent!)

N

High St.   mill

Sutton in Craven

Eastburn Crag

Intake Lane to STEETON

West Lane   Ellers

Hall Drive

The foot of a locally notorious 700ft. hill-climb

②

Summer House Farm

Valley Farm

If the ✳ footbridge is not in place, go back to cross by the concrete one.

arched bridge

footbridge

concrete bridge

footbridge ✳

Eastburn is a small village which sprang to prominence when the large hospital was built nearby. Even more modern on the 'Airedale' scene is the trunk road, and both are prominent features of the view from Eastburn Crag. The old quarry (an enormous hole) is a colourful example of the healing powers of nature.

Sutton Clough

SUTTON

shut

Long House

The clough is a hugely attractive, deep-cut wooded dell.

①

farm

KEIGHLEY

WALK 5
5¼ miles

from Oxenhope

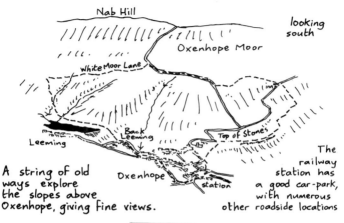

A string of old
ways explore
the slopes above
Oxenhope, giving fine views.

The
railway
station has
a good car-park,
with numerous
other roadside locations

THE WALK

From the railway station turn left up Harry Lane, cross straight over the main road and continue up the narrow and steep Dark Lane. At the first opportunity go right along a quiet back lane to emerge by Oxenhope's post office in Lowertown. Go left up the road a short distance before going right on Jew Lane. Avoid further lesser forks right until at the handful of houses at Back Leeming bear right on a level 'no through road'. This soon becomes a track, and at a house over the beck, a green lane. Take a stile behind this house and follow the left-hand wall up to a farm road by Leeming Reservoir.

Cross straight over it on another farm track to a fork, going left across another field and then leave the track as it climbs right. Continue straight on a sketchy path across several fields to drop down to a footbridge near the reservoir head. From it climb the field behind to a stile onto the moor, then head up a path to a lonesome old stile before crossing the beck on the left in its concrete runway. Now rise up the tongue to the left to reach a conduit, which can be crossed (if not jumped!) by a stile in the right-hand of two bridges. Head up the slope again to the prominent trees above to join the clear track of Sawood Lane.

Turn right along the track's generally level way, avoiding one or two lesser branches departing at sharp angles. Our track becomes known as White Moor Lane before emerging onto a surfaced lane. Turn right along this quiet road until just past the prominent mast: as a steep descent commences take a stile on the left to cross two field-tops to join a green lane. Head left to climb a little before dropping down to the *Waggon and Horses* inn on the Hebden Bridge road.

Cross straight over and down a rough track, going right at the bottom, past a farm and on to emerge onto the patch of moorland known as Stones. As the track goes sharp left take the path rising to a wall-corner to then pleasantly run along the Top of Stones. At the end turn right along an enclosed track, and when two tracks depart left at the same time (the first a drive, the second a green way) take the first one, remaining with the right-hand wall to a stile and descending to meet Shaw Lane in Oxenhope.

Turn right to the junction with the main road, and then take a surfaced path on the left, through the park to join Cross Lane just past the school. Turn down it and then right along Mill Lane to return to the railway station.

St. Mary the Virgin, Oxenhope

Stones is a prominent gritstone outcrop directly above the village, with a steep heathery drop and otherwise surrounded by green fields. Like the majority of this walk it offers impressive views of Oxenhope's environs and the rolling moors above Haworth.

HEBDEN BRIDGE
A6033
Hard Nese (Farm)
Oxenhope re-appears
Top of Stones
Stones
④
conduit
A6033
inn
Intake Lane
N
A6033
ROAD
ROAD
* mast
③
MARSH
Park
HAWORTH
station
KEIGHLEY
A6033
inn
Oxenhope

This moor-road, roughly-surfaced at the top, leads to the highest inn in West Yorkshire before dropping to Halifax

Leeming is a small mill-settlement strung along the Denholme-Oxenhope road, looking down on the latter. It has a brace of watering-holes, aside from its reservoir of 1877 which is parallel to the village.

Back Leeming
①
PO

Above White Moor Lane the moorland rises steeply to Nab Hill, with its prominent cairns standing about 1500 feet up.

Leeming
Leeming Reservoir
Nab Scar
BCH/DENHOLME

sunken and wet-escape above it
②
White Moor Lane
Harden Clough
Sawood Lane
conduit

Oxenhope's best connection with Haworth is the Keighley and Worth Valley Railway, this being the line's terminus, with a railway museum adjacent. The 5-mile line from Keighley closed in 1961 before enthusiasts stepped in to save it.

Oxenhope is a fine example of a Pennine mill community. The village sits in a basin with steep hills rising on almost all sides, through pastures to the layer of moor above. While its illustrious neighbour Haworth draws the tourists, Oxenhope takes a back seat and seems quite happy to stay largely unaltered. The squat church looks down from its lofty perch, witnessing, among other things, a now-famous annual event, the straw race. This colourful pub crawl is also a great charity fund-raiser.

WALK 6

6¼ miles

THE MONUMENTS OF EARL CRAG

from Cowling

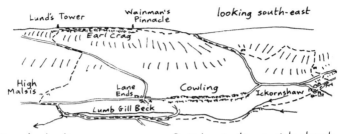

looking south-east

Lund's Tower · Wainman's Pinnacle · Earl Crag · High Malsis · Lane Ends · Cowling · Ickornshaw · Lumb Gill Beck

Lovely beck scenery contrasts with the main features of the walk, which provide breathtaking views of South Craven

Park by Cowling parish church at Ickornshaw. This is at the top end of the village and clearly visible from the main road. The best of several alternatives is parking at Lane Ends Bridge (see map).

THE WALK

From the church gate take the lane branching off opposite through the hamlet of Ickornshaw. After crossing the beck take a stile on the left and climb steeply up to another stile onto the main road. A mere 75 or so yards to the left a stile opposite takes us up a field to the farm of Lower Summer House. Two stiles keep us left of the buildings to a walled track rising behind the farm. Passing a branch right a gate is reached. It is worth going a little further on to see Lumb Gill waterfall at close hand, but our way then takes a gate to the left just before the gate on the track.

Descend by the wall to a gate in the bottom, and cross a small beck. A green way (Close Lane) climbs the opposite slope to emerge onto a narrow road at a sharp bend above a farm. Continuing uphill the road soon rises over a tract of moorland, and when a wall returns on the left (parking area) take a gate in the fence to run along the wall-side to the waiting Wainman's Pinnacle.

In view now is our next objective, Lund's Tower, and a path takes a marvellous course above the crag to it. Leave the tower by a path by the fence just before it to circumvent the cliff and join a lane. Turn down it a short distance as far as a track to Brush Farm on the right. Avoid a 'Footpath to Sutton' sign and instead descend half-left to a gate, beyond which is a short enclosed way. At the end of it simply follow the left-hand wall down through a succession of fields, eventually arriving at a gate from where a track materialises to arrive at High Malsis. Don't enter the farmyard but take a gate to reach a short row of houses. From here a drive goes down to the main road only 100 yards up from the Dog and Gun.

Our route however crosses to the path opposite and along to the junction just to the left, then follows the lane branching off for an easy ten minutes. Just beyond a branch right, we leave on a lesser lane to the left to drop down to Lane Ends Bridge. Almost immediately after crossing it, re-cross the beck on a footbridge and follow the beck upstream through park-like surroundings. Just beyond a confluence is a footbridge: cross it and follow the track away from the beck.

Around the corner is a junction of tracks at Wood House: bear right along a pleasant track, Cinder Hill Lane. N.B. a left fork at the junction would lead over the other arm of the beck and up into the centre of Cowling village. Meanwhile Cinder Hill Lane leads unerringly back – high above the beck – to emerge via a stile back onto the lane by the parish church.

Lund's Tower

Wainman's Pinnacle From Earl Crag

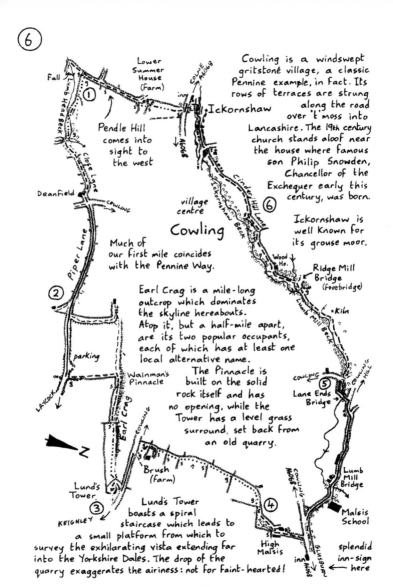

⑥

Cowling is a windswept gritstone village, a classic Pennine example, in fact. Its rows of terraces are strung along the road over 't' moss into Lancashire. The 19th century church stands aloof near the house where famous son Philip Snowden, Chancellor of the Exchequer early this century, was born.

Ickornshaw is well known for its grouse moor.

Pendle Hill comes into sight to the west

Much of our first mile coincides with the Pennine Way.

Earl Crag is a mile-long outcrop which dominates the skyline hereabouts. Atop it, but a half-mile apart, are its two popular occupants, each of which has at least one local alternative name.

The Pinnacle is built on the solid rock itself and has no opening, while the Tower has a level grass surround, set back from an old quarry.

Lund's Tower boasts a spiral staircase which leads to a small platform from which to survey the exhilarating vista extending far into the Yorkshire Dales. The drop of the quarry exaggerates the airiness: not for faint-hearted!

Fall
Lower Summer House (Farm)
Lumb Head Beck
①
Deanfield
Close Lane
Piper Lane
②
parking
LAYCOCK
Wainman's Pinnacle
Earl Crag
Brush (Farm)
Lund's Tower
③ KEIGHLEY
COLNE A6068
inn
Ickornshaw
village centre
Cowling
Cinder Hill Lane
Ickornshaw Beck
Wood Ho.
Ridge Mill Bridge (Footbridge)
Lumb Mill Beck
Kiln
COWLING
Lane Ends Bridge
COWLING HILL
Lumb Mill Bridge
④
High Malsis
inn
Malsis School
splendid inn-sign here

N

28

WALK 7
8 miles

TOP WITHINS AND HAWORTH MOOR

from Haworth

The most convenient parking is at Penistone Hill, on the moor edge above the village, but see below

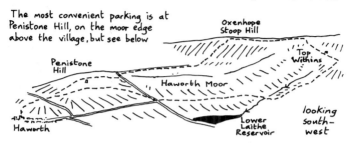

The map and description commence from the parish church, a more satisfying start in view of the walk's historical connection. Use one of the village car-parks. The Penistone Hill start saves 2 miles.

A splendid moorland ramble with a rather special objective.

THE WALK

Leave Haworth's main street by the path along the side of the parish church, then take the path behind the church, which crosses the churchyard to emerge as a flagged, enclosed way. At a branch right turn up it to join a lane on the moor edge. Cross straight over and take the path to the left: at a fork go right to contour along the hill to a car park on Penistone Hill. Go on to a junction of tracks and here take a signposted path to the right down through the heather. An unfenced road is joined, and a few yards below a wide track sets off across Haworth Moor.

This track clings to the right-hand wall for a mile, narrowing into a path to drop down to the tiny Brontë Bridge. Cross it and climb a small field to a gateway, and at a fork take the left-hand path which rises a little more before running through a series of collapsed walls and the occasional intact one. The path remains clear throughout, and beyond a tiny beck it makes a short, steep climb to join the Pennine Way at the ruin of Withins. Go left along it for a brief pull up to the rather more famous ruins of Top Withins.

After a well-earned rest continue along the path which remains level between broken walls before curving gently

29

up to the right to gain the watershed. Here we leave the Pennine Way just beyond the highest cairn, to take a sketchy path to the left alongside an unmistakeable drain. This is followed along the broad ridge for a full mile, and a modest rise onto Oxenhope Stoop Hill brings us to the corner of an inevitably collapsed wall. Turn down the side of it to begin a long descent. After an infant beck parts us from the wall an area of bracken is reached: don't be tempted by paths left or right but continue straight down, staying near the wall until a tiny beck crosses our path.

The beck is best crossed a little to the left, and after a short rise — keeping just below the heather line — the wall is rejoined to eventually emerge onto a moor road. Turn up it a few yards then take the track right which returns us to Penistone Hill. To return to Haworth bear right at a junction of tracks and continue on to the edge of a cricket ground (prominent 'pavilion'). Go left of it along a wide path which passes the Ordnance column (OSBM 11900) atop Penistone Hill to descend to merge with the outward path. Cross the lane to return to the church by the enclosed track.

The profusion of crumbling walls walls hereabouts is testament to the downfall of the small hill-farm. Several ruins can be seen from this walk.

③

South Dean Beck

Brontë Bridge
Brontë Waterfall

rebuilt 1990 – see tablet

Brontë Bridge is an attractive clapper-type bridge, but the equally famed Brontë waterfall has pushed the literary connection a little far. It allegedly occurs on the tiny beck which we cross just before the bridge: this slender trickle, which can be seen – if not recognised – from the path is no different from a thousand other tinkling becks in the neighbourhood.

②

N

Withins (ruin)

Top Withins

Spa Hill

Oxenhope Stoop Hill 455'

x = boundary stones

cairns

Dick Delf Hill

④   1490'

⑤

Footpath re-inforcement experiment ongoing here

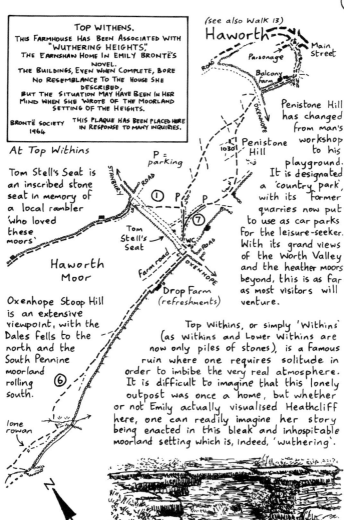

TOP WITHENS.
THIS FARMHOUSE HAS BEEN ASSOCIATED WITH "WUTHERING HEIGHTS", THE EARNSHAW HOME IN EMILY BRONTË'S NOVEL.
THE BUILDINGS, EVEN WHEN COMPLETE, BORE NO RESEMBLANCE TO THE HOUSE SHE DESCRIBED,
BUT THE SITUATION MAY HAVE BEEN IN HER MIND WHEN SHE WROTE OF THE MOORLAND SETTING OF THE HEIGHTS.

BRONTË SOCIETY 1964   THIS PLAQUE HAS BEEN PLACED HERE IN RESPONSE TO MANY INQUIRIES.

(see also Walk 13)

Haworth

Main Street

Parsonage

Balcony Farm

ROAD

OXENHOPE

Penistone Hill

1030'

STANBURY ROAD

P = parking

① P P

⑦

WC

Tom Stell's Seat

Farm road

OXENHOPE ROAD

Drop Farm (refreshments)

Haworth Moor

⑥

lone rowan

N

At Top Withins

Tom Stell's Seat is an inscribed stone seat in memory of a local rambler who loved 'these moors'.

Oxenhope Stoop Hill is an extensive viewpoint, with the Dales fells to the north and the South Pennine moorland rolling south.

Penistone Hill has changed from man's workshop to his playground. It is designated a 'country park', with its former quarries now put to use as car parks for the leisure-seeker. With its grand views of the Worth Valley and the heather moors beyond, this is as far as most visitors will venture.

Top Withins, or simply 'Withins' (as Withins and Lower Withins are now only piles of stones), is a famous ruin where one requires solitude in order to imbibe the very real atmosphere. It is difficult to imagine that this lonely outpost was once a home, but whether or not Emily actually visualised Heathcliff here, one can readily imagine her story being enacted in this bleak and inhospitable moorland setting which is, indeed, 'wuthering'.

Brontë Bridge

31

Brontë Parsonage
Museum

across :
Main Street, Haworth

Top Withins

WALK 8
4¾ miles

| GREAT EDGE AND KELBROOK MOOR |

from Black Lane Ends

An easy
circuit of
Kelbrook
Moor on
seldom-
used
ways

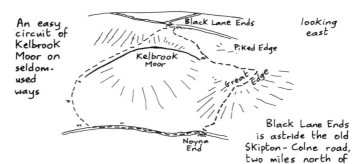

*looking
east*

Black Lane Ends
is astride the old
Skipton - Colne road,
two miles north of
Laneshaw Bridge, and is named on OS maps. Outside of the *Hare & Hounds*
car-park, the road itself is wide enough, in parts, to park safely.

| THE WALK |

Leave the road by the right side of the inn, where
a pair of gates lead into a field. Rise half-left to a stile and
across to another in a parallel wall. Bear right over the brow
of Piked Edge to a stile in the far right corner (aim for the
prominent Copy House farm beyond). A short descent to another
stile precedes an accompanying wall to the farm itself. Cross
almost straight over to a gate left of a barn, and then up a
short track into a field. It crosses to another gate before we
leave it by aiming for a stile just left of the trees ahead.

Continue this direction across two more fields to a
stile in a wall-corner. Now go right along the crest of Great
Edge, and from the next stile a long descent of the broad
ridge is made. Near the bottom an accompanying wall leads us
down to a beck. Follow it upstream to a plank footbridge, crossing
to a stile in the fence just across it, then rise up the slope
behind to a stile onto a green track. This leads left onto the
narrow lane at Noyna End.

This traffic-free back road is followed right, over
the brow of the hill and on a very gradual descent towards
Kelbrook village. Just as it is about to drop more steeply go
along an enclosed track to the right. It is signposted Harden

34

New Hall Farm and leads unerringly to it.

Keep right of the farm to a stile in a fence just beyond it, then aim straight across two trackless pastures before bearing right up the slope to Harden Clough. Pass to the rear (left) of the house, and emerge onto the old lane that is its drive. Cross straight over to a footbridge. A slim path breasts the steep slope opposite Kelbrook Wood, thence more gently after a stile to Scald Bank. A track leads away from the house to peter out at a wall-corner: now take a stile in front and maintain the direction to cross a field to a collapsed wall. Rise by the left-hand wall to a stile from where the inn reappears at our feet. Drop down to complete the walk via the gates through which it began.

Kelbrook Wood is a beautiful mixed woodland on a steep sheltered slope under the moor.

Black Lane Ends

CARLETON

inn

COLNE

1155'

Harden Clough (4)

Scald Bank

Kelbrook Wood

Pendle Hill appears

Piked Edge

Harden New Hall (farm)

Kelbrook Moor

Copy House (farm)

Piked Edge does not entirely live up to its name!

Kelbrook Moor tops a rounded hill which shows its steepest face to the north, above Harden New Hall. It is not, however, too forthcoming as regards access to walkers.

(3)

Thick Bank (farm)

moor

KELBROOK

Hard Clough (farm)

Cob Lane

This walk is entirely in Lancashire, although Black Lane Ends is within a half-mile of North Yorkshire.

(1)

1130'

Z

Great Edge

Arrival on Great Edge signals splendid views westward, including Boulsworth Hill, the Lancashire moors, Pendle Hill, the Bowland Fells, Ingleborough and Penyghent.

Throstle Nest

(2)

Noyna End

FOULRIDGE

On dropping off Great Edge, Colne and the Foulridge reservoirs are at your feet.

35

WALK 9

4 miles

from Stanbury

An easy to follow exploration
of the Ponden off-shoot
of the Worth Valley.

looking
south

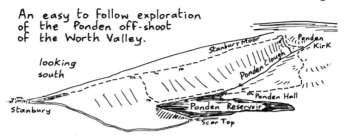

There is parking
for a few cars at the bus terminus (Hob Hill) at the western
end of the village. An alternative start would be to cross
the embankment of Ponden Reservoir and park on the very
rough and wide lane. This would also shorten the walk.

THE WALK

Leave the road at Hob Hill by the narrow lane
rising to the left. At an early fork go right, and after it
has deteriorated into a rough track it forks again. Now go
left on a wide track which rises gently before accompanying
a wall along a finger of moorland to Far Slack Farm. Take a
stile in the fence to the left and follow a thin path by the wall,
continuing straight on when the wall drops away. On gaining the
steeper edge of Ponden Clough avoid a branch sloping down to
the right and continue along the top (beware steep drops!) to
cross the first of the two feeder becks.
While an alternative path (see opposite) makes a rough
descent here, a better path remains high-level, contouring above
the clough and passing the outcrop of Ponden Kirk to reach the
second feeder beck in a lovely setting. Continue along the clough
edge, dropping slightly and then being deflected away by a wall
to descend to a lone barn. A trod to the left runs down to a
broad track: follow this right, past a wall-corner and on to a
gate to leave the moor. Descend a farm road to a junction above
Ponden Reservoir, then go right, passing Ponden Hall and dropping to
run the length of the reservoir. At the end take a track right: it
quickly rises as a green way to a stile onto a rough access road.
Go left to rejoin the outward route and retrace those steps.

Ponden Hall

Ponden Hall is a lovely structure perched high above the reservoir. It dates from the 17th century, and was reputedly the Thrushcross Grange of Emily Brontë's *Wuthering Heights*. Today it offers accommodation and refreshments.

Stanbury

At Stanbury worked Timmy Feather, thought to have been the last hand-loom weaver. He died in 1910.

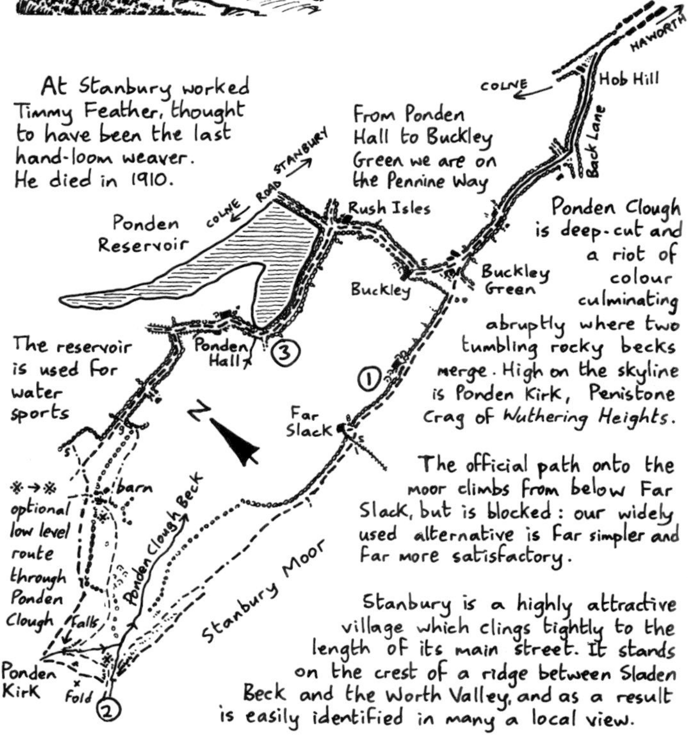

From Ponden Hall to Buckley Green we are on the Pennine Way

Ponden Clough is deep-cut and a riot of colour culminating abruptly where two tumbling rocky becks merge. High on the skyline is Ponden Kirk, Penistone Crag of *Wuthering Heights*.

The reservoir is used for water sports

The official path onto the moor climbs from below Far Slack, but is blocked: our widely used alternative is far simpler and far more satisfactory.

Stanbury is a highly attractive village which clings tightly to the length of its main street. It stands on the crest of a ridge between Sladen Beck and the Worth Valley, and as a result is easily identified in many a local view.

(Map labels:) Stanbury · HAWORTH · COLNE · Hob Hill · Back Lane · STANBURY · Rush Isles · Buckley · Buckley Green · COLNE Road · Ponden Reservoir · Ponden Hall · ③ · ① · Far Slack · N · barn · ✱→✱ optional low level route through Ponden Clough · falls · Ponden Clough Beck · Stanbury Moor · Ponden Kirk · Fold · ②

WALK 10

| GOIT STOCK WOOD AND HARDEN MOOR |

6 miles   from Harden

A brilliantly colourful walk, with a
memorable contrast
of woodland
and open
moor

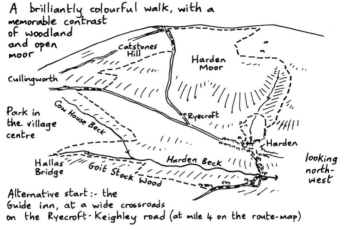

Alternative start :- the
Guide inn, at a wide crossroads
on the Ryecroft-Keighley road (at mile 4 on the route-map)

| THE WALK |

From the staggered crossroads by the post office turn
along the Wilsden road and descend to cross Harden Beck. Up
the steep slope behind avoid a bend in the main road by the
parallel Mill Hill Top. On rejoining the road go past a garden
centre to a row of cottages, and immediately after take a
stile on the right. A good level path soon enters the trees
and runs along the top of the wood to be confronted rather
surprisingly by a pylon. Just beyond it the best path forks
right to descend to Harden Beck, while the right-of-way
crosses back into a field before re-entering the wood to drop
more steeply to the beck. A wide path heads upstream to
Goit Stock Falls, where a handrail assists in surmounting
the cliff to continue upstream to Hallas Bridge.

Cross the bridge and leave the track immediately
on a short path up to a stile on the right. A small field is
crossed to re-enter woods on a splendid level path. On finally
leaving, a large field is crossed to Cow House Beck, and up the
slope behind we turn sharp left at the first wall. This right-
hand wall is accompanied on a good path above Cow House Beck

38

all the way to join the Cullingworth–Harden road. Go right a short distance then left up a delightful green way known as Dolphin Lane, to rise to the moor of Catstones Hill. Head to the left on a good path until almost at a gate, then fork right on a path up to join another rising from the gate. This path climbs through long-defunct quarries to then rise more gently across the moor and onto another road. This is now followed left up to the crossroads by the *Guide*.

Do not be tempted by any of the roads, however, but take the wide track on the right and follow it all the way to a T-junction of tracks. Here take a 'gap-stile' in the fence on the right to accompany a superb partly-flagged old track striking across Harden Moor. At a crossroads go left to a gritstone outcrop then down to a wall-corner, remaining with the wall to the head of Deep Cliff Hole.

At the path's lowest point (stile on the left), fork right on a thinner, level path which runs between the moor and the steep drop through the trees. Avoid any lesser forks, and on arrival at a wall-corner the path soon drops down to leave the trees and crosses a small field to meet an enclosed track. Turn right along it and as it starts to rise soon after crossing the beck, take a stile in front to cross a field to Spring Farm. Head away between the buildings but just before reaching Spring House take a narrow, enclosed footpath down to the left.

The path soon accompanies the beck to a mill-yard. Continue straight on to rejoin the main road in the centre of Harden village, by way of a little street known as *Back 'o The Mill*.

Goit Stock Falls

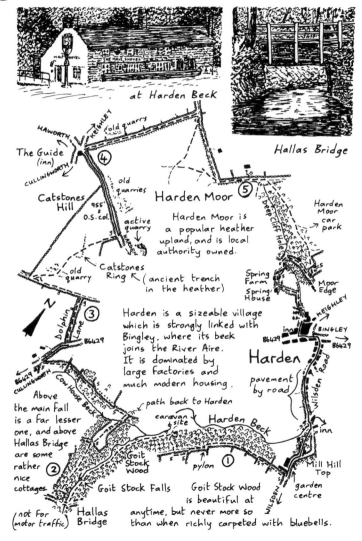

at Harden Beck

Hallas Bridge

HAWORTH
KEIGHLEY
old quarry

The Guide
(inn)
CULLINGWORTH

④

Catstones
Hill

955'
O.S. col.

active
quarry

old
quarries

Harden Moor

⑤

Harden Moor is
a popular heather
upland, and is local
authority owned.

Harden
Moor
car
park

Deep Cliff Hole

Spring
Farm
Spring
House

Moor
Edge

KEIGHLEY

old
quarry

Catstones
Ring ← (ancient trench
in the heather)

inn
B6429

BINGLEY

B6429

N

③

Dolphin Lane

B6429

Harden is a sizeable village
which is strongly linked with
Bingley, where its beck
joins the River Aire.
It is dominated by
large factories and
much modern housing.

Harden

pavement
by road

Wilsden Road

B6429
CULLINGWORTH

Cow House Beck

Above
the main fall
is a far lesser
one, and above
Hallas Bridge
are some
rather
nice
cottages.

②

path back to Harden

caravan
& site

Harden Beck

inn

Goit
Stock
Wood

pylon

①

Mill Hill
Top

garden
centre

(not for
motor traffic)

Hallas
Bridge

Goit Stock Falls

Goit Stock Wood
is beautiful at
anytime, but never more so
than when richly carpeted with bluebells.

WILSDEN

WALK 11

5 miles

BOULSWORTH HILL

from Trawden

A clear day is essential for this straightforward ascent of a supreme viewpoint.

looking south-east

Park on the cul-de-sac lane between the parish church and the mill at Hollin Hall.

A start from the mill saves a mile of walking from the total.

THE WALK

The road from the church narrows immediately after the mill, and we follow it in its new guise as a country lane until a sharp bend to the left. Now go straight on along a farm track, keeping left of the buildings to a gate at the rear. A wide track heads away to another gate then descends to cross a beck. Here a tiny detour is recommended down the opposite bank for a splendid view of Lumb Spout waterfall.

From the beck head directly away up a conspicuous dry groove to a scattering of trees, a little beyond which is a stile. From it a wall rises away to another stile onto a wide track alongside the intake wall. Go right a few yards then head up a concrete waterworks access road, which soon terminates at a covered reservoir. From here a fairly clear path strikes directly uphill, a series of marker posts serving to confirm the route. Eventually the broad ridge of Boulsworth Hill is joined at Little Chair Stones, and the path now swings right to follow it to the Ordnance column atop Lad Law, summit of the hill.

The descent commences immediately, with a line of posts again marking the way down to rejoin the wide track along the moor-edge. Go left a few yards only and leave it by a stile in the wall, then head down a vague path on

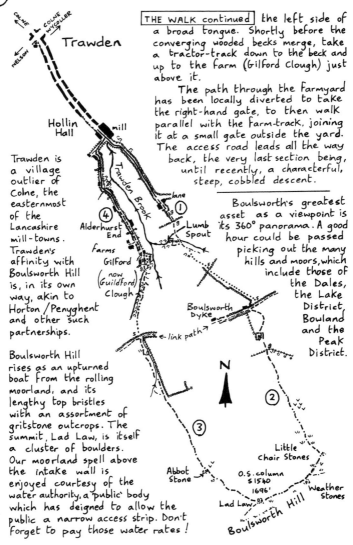

Trawden

Hollin Hall — mill

Trawden Brook

Alderhurst End

④

Gilford (now (Guildford) Clough)

Farms

lane

①

Lumb Spout

Boulsworth Dyke

← link path →

N

②

Little Chair Stones

Abbot Stone

③

O.S. column S1540 1696'

Lad Law

Weather Stones

Boulsworth Hill

THE WALK continued the left side of a broad tongue. Shortly before the converging wooded becks merge, take a tractor-track down to the beck and up to the farm (Gilford Clough) just above it.

The path through the farmyard has been locally diverted to take the right-hand gate, to then walk parallel with the farm-track, joining it at a small gate outside the yard. The access road leads all the way back, the very last section being, until recently, a characterful, steep, cobbled descent.

Boulsworth's greatest asset as a viewpoint is its 360° panorama. A good hour could be passed picking out the many hills and moors, which include those of the Dales, the Lake District, Bowland and the Peak District.

Trawden is a village outlier of Colne, the easternmost of the Lancashire mill-towns. Trawden's affinity with Boulsworth Hill is, in its own way, akin to Horton/Penyghent and other such partnerships.

Boulsworth Hill rises as an upturned boat from the rolling moorland, and its lengthy top bristles with an assortment of gritstone outcrops. The summit, Lad Law, is itself a cluster of boulders. Our moorland spell above the intake wall is enjoyed courtesy of the water authority, a public body which has deigned to allow the public a narrow access strip. Don't forget to pay those water rates !

Lumb Spout

WALK 12

4¼ miles

A simple circuit of Cononley's own hill, with superb views both up and down the Aire valley

Parking can be found on the Main Street, at its widest part near the New Inn. or in the small car park where Meadow Lane meets the Main Street.

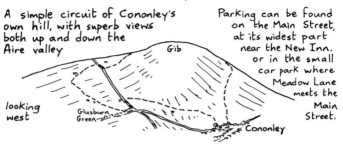

looking west

THE WALK

From the bridge by the post office walk up Main Street past the *New Inn* and leave it by a rough track just before the Institute. It climbs to Town Head Farm, but we leave it at the sharp bend before the farm, continuing up a walled green track. At the top turn right and accompany a wall rising to Great Gib. Pass left of the building to a stile onto a track, leaving it at the next building by a stile on the left. Rise half-right to another stile in the corner, then head away to join a track which heads past the remains of mining activity. Now maintain a level course and the track improves to approach Manor Farm. Well before reaching its confines, however, head up to the left (pathless) to follow a wall away to a stile in the top corner. Now descend half-right over moorland to another corner-stile, and follow the left-hand wall away to the Cross Hills–Lothersdale road.

Turn right along this very straight road until a farm road heads off to the left. Don't follow it however, but opt for the track running down the wall-side. At two gates take the left one to descend to West Closes. Turn left along its access track to pass several farms before emerging onto Green Lane. Go left up to a junction and then left again up the Lothersdale road.

The road is soon vacated at a stile on the right just before a farm. A good track runs to a kissing-gate, past a former reservoir and across two small pastures at an angle. A large rough pasture is descended to Gibside Farm: remain above the wall however (no clear path) until a stile in it leads down a narrow pasture onto a track. Just below is the road leading left to the village centre.

Cononley is a traditional Airedale mill village, with its centre hiding many attractive cottages (+2 inns): an amazing terrace is strung along the Cross Hills road. Unique in this book and only yards off-route are the restored workings of a lead mine, with a chimney and a Cornish style engine house.

Cononley lead mine

The hardest part of this walk is quickly accomplished, for on reaching Great Gib virtually all the climbing is over. Note the two attractive wooded gills across to the right, while ascending.

From above Gibside farm the Aire valley can be seen stretching for many a mile. Across it are Rombalds, Farnhill and Skipton Moors, while behind Skipton itself rise the shapely tops of Flasby Fell, and also Barden Moor. Villages on show include Bradley, Farnhill and Cross Hills.

Cononley

CARLETON

inn

TO A629

LOTHERSDALE

Town Head (Farm)

N

Great Gib
Little Gib

Gib Side

④

CROSS HILLS

chimney (prominent in distant views) ×

Gibside (farm)

imposing lead-mining remains

①

8900' Gib summit (approx)

Manor Farm

The Gib's steep slopes face east across the Aire Valley

LOTHERSDALE

short-cut

disused concrete reservoir

CONONLEY

Well House (farm)

The more direct access track through Manor Farm is no longer a public path.

Well Spring Farm

③

CROSS HILLS

Between miles ① and ③ Earl Crag fills the skyline to the south. The foreground is beautifully wooded, with the tower of Malsis school rising through the trees.

②

West Closes (farm)

Scott House
Green House
(Farms)

Binns Lane

GLUSBURN

Glusburn Green

some desirable residences hereabouts

WALK 13 | BROW MOOR AND BRIDGEHOUSE BECK |

4¾ miles   from Haworth

Good beckside and moorland scenery, with the added
attraction of the Worth Valley Railway in close proximity

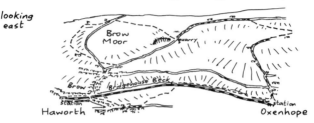

looking
east

The walk begins at Haworth station — there is parking in the
railway yard. Otherwise park at the top of the village and walk
down through Haworth Park to the railway station.
A very good alternative start is Oxenhope station. This has
the advantage of dealing with the steep climbing at the outset.

| THE WALK |

*opposite: Haworth
  parish church*

From the railway station cross the footbridge over
the line and go left along Belle Isle Road. At the far end
cross the main road and rise up a rough lane (Ivy Bank Lane),
turning left at the top to leave Haworth along Sun Street. After
a slight rise take the second stile on the left (by a gate) and
follow a flagged path away. Continue down the next field to
join an enclosed track at the bottom corner. It drops down to
pass under the railway and over a footbridge: turn right to
accompany Bridgehouse Beck upstream. Cross it at a footbridge
and continue through a farmyard, leaving by its access track
to another bridge. Here a wicket-gate on the right sandwiches
us between beck and railway: at another footbridge cross the
beck again, and after a couple more upstream stiles the path
emerges into a mill yard. Oxenhope station is just down to
the right.
Our route continues up the lane to the left (Harry
Lane), straight over the main road and up the narrow, surfaced
Dark Lane to its demise into a rough track. Just beyond, and
now on the level, a ruined farm is reached. Here we leave the

track by doubling back to a stile on the left. From it avoid the path by the left-hand wall and take a less-clear path to rise gradually on a tiny heather ridge above an old sunken way. The path maintains its gentle rise to eventually meet a wall, then accompanying it up to a stile onto Black Moor Lane.

Go left along this quiet lane for nearly ¾ miles, and when the right-hand wall rejoins us just before a quarry and a steep drop, leave the road alongside the wall striking up to the right. An initially inauspicious start soon improves into a good track, remaining with the wall to cross Brow Moor and descend to a road. Cross straight over and down the rough track of Hardgate Lane. After a steep drop past old quarries it levels out at some buildings: here take a stile on the left and follow a wall away.

On drawing level with a small reservoir the path rises across a patch of moorland, soon being met by a wall again to arrive at a large modern hotel. Its drive leads up onto the road over Brow Moor. Turn right for 50 or so yards then take the second good path striking across the moor. It descends gradually back onto Black Moor Road at a farm. Turn right a short distance then take a short path left to cut a corner off the road. Just below is Hebden Road (A6033): cross over and down the extremely steep Brow Road to emerge back at the environs of the railway. Haworth station is just along to the right - on Station Road!

Haworth ceased to be just another village in the 19th century when the fame of the Brontës spread, though it took until relatively recently to become a full-blown tourist honeypot. The focal point is the cobbled main street, lined with shops and climbing steeply to the parish church. Surrounded by inns, only its tower remains from the Brontës' day, but hidden behind it is the parsonage, now a museum of its former occupants. Only minutes away is open moorland, while back down the main street is the second major attraction, namely the Keighley and Worth Valley Railway. Although this preserved steam line runs from Keighley to Oxenhope, Haworth station, with its goods yard, is the hub of things. Interestingly, the railway actually leaves the Worth Valley near Oakworth to follow Bridgehouse Beck past Haworth to Oxenhope, a reminder of its original purpose, to serve the mills.

Haworth

A = to Main Street

KEIGHLEY B6142

station

park

KEIGHLEY A6033

hotel

④ reservoir

Brow Moor

First wind-turbine in the area (1992)

x active quarry

BRADFORD B6144

A6033

③

Oxenhope

Bridgehouse Beck

① charming little stone footbridge

N

Black Moor Road

Both Haworth and Oxenhope are seen at their best from the east side of the valley with both churches prominent. At Haworth the houses seem to clamber over each other up the main street, while Oxenhope rests more sedately beneath a backdrop of high moorland.

From the top of Brow Moor there is a surprise view of Pendle Hill peeking over the pass at the very head of the Worth Valley.

The first surprise view (on a clear day!) comes on first gaining Black Moor Road, for to the north-west above Oakworth Moor the shapely outlines of both Ingleborough and Penyghent can be distinguished 28 miles distant.

station (terminus)

A6033

Dark Lane

Upwood

Bentley Hey

Oxenhope
(see also Walk 5)

this ruin is as sad as it is photogenic

②

WALK 14
5¾ miles

ST. IVES AND DRUID'S ALTAR

from Bingley

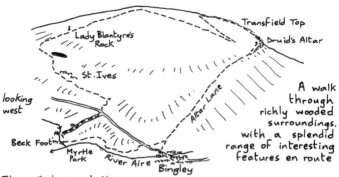

A walk
through
richly wooded
surroundings,
with a splendid
range of interesting
features en route

The walk begins at the
parish church at the Keighley end of Main Street (parking alongside).
An excellent alternative is to start at St. Ives (good parking). There
are entrances on the Bingley-Harden and Harden-Keighley roads.

THE WALK

From the church leave the Main Street at the traffic
lights and take the Harden road over the Aire, then leave it
immediately by a steep path up through the trees on the right.
It soon joins a rough track (Altar Lane) which leads seemingly
endlessly uphill, though the gradient does ease up as height is
gained. After about a mile the plantation on the right drops away
and directly in front are the rocks at the Druid's Altar. At this
point leave the track and take the path across to the edge.

The path runs along the top of the crags, crossing
a track to use a stile to continue along the equally enjoyable
Transfield Top. When a stile appears on the left make use of
it to head half-right to a wall-corner, then turn sharp left to
follow a vague track towards a pylon. Go on through a gateway
to a stile back onto Altar Lane. Follow it back almost to where
we left it, but as the Druid's Altar is neared take a stile on the
right to enter the St. Ives estate.

Head right along a good path which remains near the
wall until confronted by a lesser wall. Here it turns left to begin
a long descent to Lady Blantyre's Rock, and down still further

before swinging left to run alongside Coppice Pond. Now the road through the estate is crossed to another path which runs below the mansion itself. On meeting the estate road again either remain on it or take a path sharp right to drop to a path running along the edge of the wood. Go left along it to rejoin the road at a lodge, then head right on it to leave very shortly after along a path into trees on the left, soon joining the Bingley-Harden road.

Cross, with the utmost caution, this frequently busy road and escape with the greatest of relief down the peaceful Beckfoot Lane. At the bottom it becomes a rough track, and just beyond is Beckfoot Bridge with adjacent ford. Do not be tempted by either but take a stile on the left. A path crosses a meadow and up to a lonely house above the River Aire, going right of it to a stile to run along the top of a wood.

The path soon descends to a riverside pasture and a footbridge over the Aire. If starting from Bingley this could be crossed to finish the walk through Myrtle Park, but alternatively remain on this bank until a wide path heads into the nearby trees to soon rejoin the road. Ireland Bridge where our walk began is only a couple of minutes down to the right. A minute of traffic can be avoided by heading up the rough lane opposite (the start of Altar Lane - which will be the route anyway if St. Ives was the start-point). To return to Bingley re-use the steep path down through the trees.

Lady Blantyre's Rock

William Ferrand Monument

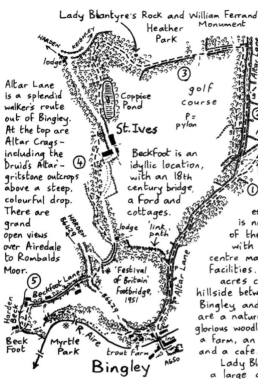

Lady Blantyre's Rock and William Ferrand Monument

Heather Park

➤ Z

HARDEN ← KEIGHLEY

lodge

Altar Lane

Coppice Pond

③

golf course

P = pylon

② Transfield Top

St. Ives

Altar Lane is a splendid walker's route out of Bingley. At the top are Altar Crags – including the Druid's Altar – gritstone outcrops above a steep, colourful drop. There are grand open views over Airedale to Rombalds Moor.

④

Beckfoot is an idyllic location, with an 18th century bridge, a ford and cottages.

Druid's Altar

①

lodge 'link path'

HARDEN B6429

Altar Lane

⑤ Beckfoot Lane

B6429

'Festival of Britain' footbridge, 1951

Harden Beck

Beck Foot

Myrtle Park

R. Aire

trout farm

A650

Bingley

Bingley is a bustling industrial town which has retained many of its pleasing old corners, notably the environs of the parish church: at the other end of the Main Street, however, is a contrasting example of what modern architects can churn out. In the spacious park is the Town Hall, a Georgian house, while nearby is the Market Hall, recently returned to its rightful place. The Leeds-Liverpool Canal flows through the town, while the Aire keeps strictly to the west, enabling us to escape immediately into the countryside.

The country estate of St. Ives is now in the hands of the local authority, with a turf research centre making use of the facilities. The hundreds of acres cover much of the hillside between Harden and Bingley, and within its walls are a nature trail through glorious woodland, a golf course, a farm, an extensive moor and a cafe and play area.

Lady Blantyre's Rock is a large gritstone boulder where the lady in question often came to sojourn. After her death in 1875, her son-in-law William Ferrand placed an inscribed tablet here. Being a famous dignitary himself, the adjacent noble obelisk was erected after his death in 1889.

WALK 15

4 miles

from Lothersdale

A rich variety of paths and green lanes guide us up and down the not so humble hills watching over lovely Lothersdale

Park on the main street in the vicinity of the inn

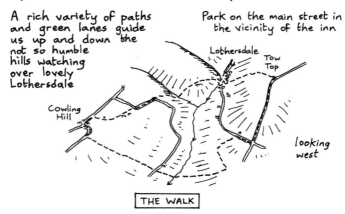

THE WALK

From the inn head east along the main street past the mill, and at the foot of the slope, after the buildings, use a gate on the left to head up a walled track. After a brief taste of freedom it becomes enclosed again, and just 50 yards after joining the rough Tow Top Lane leave it by a stile on the right. Accompany the wall away, turning left at the end to a stile onto a road. Go right to a crossroads and then right again towards Lothersdale (no, we've not finished so soon). At the first farm take a stile on the left and descend by a wall. From the bottom corner cross to another just behind it, then traverse two field-tops to Leys House, emerging between the buildings onto a lane.

Turn right to descend a green lane to a footbridge over Leys Beck, then up the other side, crossing a surfaced lane and continuing up to eventually join another lane. Turn right up to Cowling Hill, and leave at a bend along a drive opposite the graveyard. Just before Greenburn Laithe take a stile on the left and follow the wall away, crossing at a gateway and continuing on a track to Overhouse Farm, joining a lane just above it.

Turn down this narrow lane to a stile at the next bend, crossing to a tiny beck before descending two fields to cross Surgill Beck. From the gate behind it head directly away to rise towards Woodhead Farm. Follow its access road away until it parts company with the wall. With Lothersdale now at your feet descend with

the wall to a stile and then steps down towards the road.
        Instead of joining the road immediately, preferably
finish by going right on a path by the beck to pass via
cottages to the mill-yard, then sharp left to the road and inn.

        Lothersdale is a highly attractive village strung along
a quiet lane, well off the beaten track. Its seclusion in among
the hills did not prevent the arrival of the mill age – note the
striking chimney. The church stands high and isolated on the
road to the large house of Stone Gappe. Here, briefly, Charlotte
Brontë was governess, and
it became the Gateshead
Hall of Jane Eyre.

In a nearby
quarry notable
prehistoric bones
have been
unearthed.

Lothersdale

Note
the old
sundial
on the
wall of
Woodhead.
The farm
caters well
for Pennine
Wayfarers,
with whom we
share the final
mile of our walk.
(Not one of the
PW's more
eroded sections!)

Cowling Hill is an
exposed farming hamlet
accessible only by narrow winding lanes. A
Baptist chapel stands surrounded by barns.

ESLACK
CARLETON

Tow
Top

The stile at Tow Top marks
the end of the first climb,
and is a fine viewpoint. At
the next stile, Barden
Moor and Simons Seat
come into sight to
the north-east.

On joining
the lane note
the chimney atop the
Gib (1 mile east) and the
lead mining
remains on
its near
slope
(see Walk 12)

①

Stone
Gappe

CONONLEY
CROSSHILLS

guidepost still
recalling the
West Riding

BLACK
LANE
ENDS
inn
mill
PO

a classic
birds-eye
view

Woodhead
(farm)

Surgill
Beck

Overhouse
(farm)

③

BLACK LANE
ENDS

The approach to Woodhead
is alongside a sunken lane.

Leys Beck to Cowling Hill
is an uninterrupted climb,
with good views to Cowling
and Earl Crag and its
monuments near the
end of the
climb.

Greenburn
Laithe

**Cowling
Hill**

COWLING

Leys
House

Leys
Beck

②

GLUSBURN

GLUSBURN

N

Initially rough,
this narrow way
soon opens out
into a lovely
green track,
with a good
view north of
the frontage of
Stone Gappe.

WALK 16

4½ miles

from Wycoller

Easy walking to visit the
many interesting features
of the Wycoller valley

looking north-east

Herder's Inn

Foster's
Leap

Wycoller   Wycoller Beck

Use the car
park at the
entrance to the village.
A good alternative start is
the car-park on the Haworth—Colne road, west of the inn.

THE WALK

From the car park take the lane into the village,
and on arriving at the unmistakeable central 'scene' cross the
packhorse bridge by the ford and climb the stone steps up
the grass bank behind the ruined hall. From a stile at the
top a wide path rises up the field: on approaching a deep
sunken stage (the connection with the Haworth Road car park),
go right to a stile, and cross a couple of fields. After
the next stile the path forks, and here opt for the one
slanting up to the left.

Beyond a collapsed wall continue up to a stile in
the next wall, and just beyond it cross straight over a farm
road to the rocks of Foster's Leap. Head straight along the
top of the outcrops, soon with an accompanying wall. Remain
alongside it well beyond the rocks, until having lost a little
height, a stile in the wall appears: the Herders Inn is now
just above us. Rise half-left to a barn, and two small gates
to its left lead in quick succession to the inn's car park.

Turn right (passing the hostelry?) and remain on
the road almost three-quarters of a mile as it traverses the
edge of rough moorland. After the last building it swings to
the left sharply, and just beyond leave it by a gate on the
right. A good track commences the downhill return. After an
interruption by a brief climb leave the moor-edge track for one
branching right. It descends to Parson Lee Farm before a level
return to Wycoller, with Wycoller Beck as constant companion.

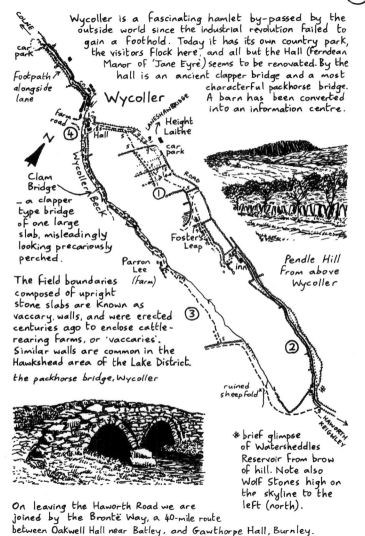

Wycoller is a fascinating hamlet by-passed by the outside world since the industrial revolution failed to gain a foothold. Today it has its own country park, the visitors flock here, and all but the Hall (Ferndean Manor of 'Jane Eyre) seems to be renovated. By the hall is an ancient clapper bridge and a most characterful packhorse bridge. A barn has been converted into an information centre.

Colne

car park

Footpath↗ alongside lane

Wycoller

farm road

④ Hall

LANESHAW BRIDGE

Height Laithe

car park

N ↙

Wycoller Beck

Clam Bridge
– a clapper type bridge of one large slab, misleadingly looking precariously perched.

ROAD

①

Foster's Leap

Pendle Hill from above Wycoller

Parson Lee (farm)

inn

The field boundaries composed of upright stone slabs are known as vaccary walls, and were erected centuries ago to enclose cattle-rearing farms, or 'vaccaries'. Similar walls are common in the Hawkshead area of the Lake District.

③

②

the packhorse bridge, Wycoller

ruined sheepfold

TO HAWORTH / KEIGHLEY

* brief glimpse of Watersheddles Reservoir from brow of hill. Note also Wolf Stones high on the skyline to the left (north).

On leaving the Haworth Road we are joined by the Brontë Way, a 40-mile route between Oakwell Hall near Batley, and Gawthorpe Hall, Burnley.

—Wycoller Hall——

——Boulsworth Hill from Foster's Leap—

WALK 17 | KEIGHLEY MOOR AND NEWSHOLME DEAN

7 miles — from Goose Eye

A walk of immense variety and colourful
surroundings, from the steep, wooded slopes
of the Dean to the
wide open moor

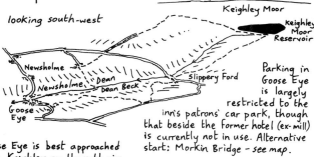

looking south-west

Keighley Moor

Keighley Moor Reservoir

Newsholme
Newsholme Dean
Dean Beck
Slippery Ford
Goose Eye

Parking in
Goose Eye
is largely
restricted to the
inn's patrons' car park, though
that beside the former hotel (ex-mill)
is currently not in use. Alternative
start: Morkin Bridge - see map.

Goose Eye is best approached
from Keighley or Haworth via
Oakworth, or via Laycock also from Keighley. Either way is interesting!

THE WALK

From the *Turkey* inn face the car-park and turn
left along the road, leaving it by a rough track on the left
after a short row of cottages. At an early junction take the
sharp turn up to the left, and before the track culminates at
a house fork right on a path. This enclosed green way leads
onto a farm track which is followed left down to Newsholme
Dean. Leave it however at the first building, by a gate on the
right from where a track runs along to another gate. Fork
right up the pasture on a green track which climbs to join
a partly-paved one at a bend. Continue up until it swings
right to emerge onto a lane.

Follow this lane only a few yards left, then take
a farm track left again. On reaching the rear of the building
(holiday cottages) use a gate on the right, and cross the bottom of
the field to a stile. Cross a tiny stream and then turn left
to contour round the slope before aiming for the farm which
appears ahead. After a short climb to it, pass along the front and
straight across a field to a stile. Follow a wall away and when

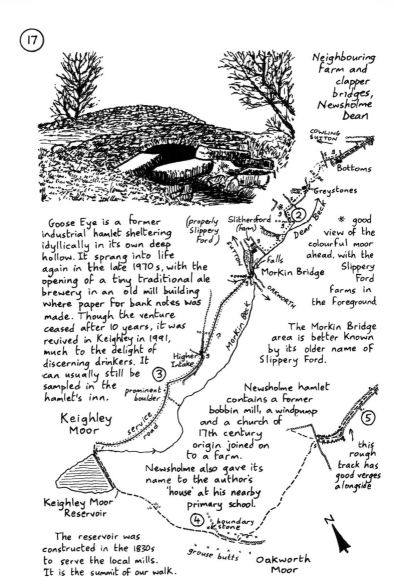

Neighbouring farm and clapper bridges, Newsholme Dean

COWLING SUTTON

Bottoms

Greystones

②

Slitherford (farm)
(properly Slippery Ford)

Dean Beck

SUTTON

falls
Morkin Bridge

OAKWORTH

Morkin Beck

Higher Intake

③

prominent boulder

Keighley Moor

service road

Keighley Moor Reservoir

④ boundary stone

grouse butts

Oakworth Moor

⑤

this rough track has good verges alongside

N

* good view of the colourful moor ahead, with the Slippery Ford farms in the foreground.

The Morkin Bridge area is better known by its older name of Slippery Ford.

Goose Eye is a former industrial hamlet sheltering idyllically in its own deep hollow. It sprang into life again in the late 1970s, with the opening of a tiny traditional ale brewery in an old mill building where paper for bank notes was made. Though the venture ceased after 10 years, it was revived in Keighley in 1991, much to the delight of discerning drinkers. It can usually still be sampled in the hamlet's inn.

Newsholme hamlet contains a former bobbin mill, a windpump and a church of 17th century origin joined on to a farm. Newsholme also gave its name to the author's 'house' at his nearby primary school.

The reservoir was constructed in the 1830s to serve the local mills. It is the summit of our walk.

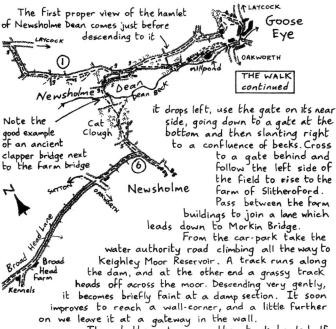

The first proper view of the hamlet of Newsholme Dean comes just before descending to it ↓

↑ LAYCOCK

Goose Eye

← LAYCOCK

① millpond

OAKWORTH

THE WALK continued

Newsholme Dean Dean Beck

Note the good example of an ancient clapper bridge next to the farm bridge

Cat Clough

⑥

Newsholme

SUTTON OAKWORTH

N

Broad Head Lane

Broad Head Farm

Kennels

it drops left, use the gate on its near side, going down to a gate at the bottom and then slanting right to a confluence of becks. Cross to a gate behind and follow the left side of the field to rise to the farm of Slitheroford. Pass between the farm buildings to join a lane which leads down to Morkin Bridge.

From the car-park take the water authority road climbing all the way to Keighley Moor Reservoir. A track runs along the dam, and at the other end a grassy track heads off across the moor. Descending very gently, it becomes briefly faint at a damp section. It soon improves to reach a wall-corner, and a little further on we leave it at a gateway in the wall.

Through the gateway another track heads half right to the third in a row of grouse butts, and keeping just left of it a slim green path heads off left through the heather. It remains generally clear all the way to a stile where a farm access road enters a rough lane. Head along this enclosed way throughout its entire length, becoming properly surfaced at a farm before eventually meeting another lane. Cross over and along another enclosed track as far as the first bend. Just along to the right the hamlet of Newsholme can be explored.

Our route, however, takes a path left at a bend in the track, and runs on to a stile high above the Dean before it drops steeply down Cat Clough. Keep straight down to a stile and then across to a bridge beyond which a track is joined to return to Newsholme Dean. Immediately after the last building go right on a hidden path, alongside a wall before dropping towards the beck. Ignore a footbridge and continue downstream, passing the old mill pond then crossing the beck to join the road at Goose Eye.

WALK 18

4½ miles

CARLETON GLEN AND RAMSHAW

from Carleton

A pleasant contrast
between wooded
beck and
open
country

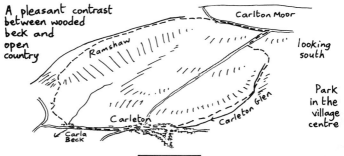

Carlton Moor

looking
south

Park
in the
village
centre

Ramshaw

Carleton Glen

Carleton

Carla
Beck

THE WALK

From the inn in the centre of the village take the Colne road (west) past the mill, and just before the last house on the left turn up a little street called The Wend. After a couple of short terraces it becomes a rough track, crossing a gill and swinging right to run parallel with the same wooded beck. After becoming unenclosed the farm track continues through several fields to end at a pronounced bend in the beck. Turn left and follow it upstream, keeping on the rim of the steep, wooded slope. Towards the top of the field close in on the beck to locate a stile in the beckside fence, here crossing the beck to climb the opposite bank.

Resume the upstream journey to a stile, then bear to the right across the field to rejoin the main beck at a gate. Beyond it descend to the beck and cross it along with a forlorn companion wall. Again head up the slope opposite and upstream to a stile, then rise to another stile in front of the farm visible ahead. Without entering its confines turn left to a gate, descending to cross the beck's beginnings and then rising with the left-hand wall to a gate. After a little dampness a path heads left to arrive at a gate onto a lane.

Turn up the lane to a T-junction and then go left, staying on the road past a lesser right fork and soon arriving at a farm track to Tewit Cote. Turn left along it and then branch left to a stile in the far corner. The rough moorland of Burnt Hill is entered, and the right-hand wall is followed to a stile from where a left-hand wall takes over. In the slight dip just beyond take a stile in the wall to return it to our right. A narrow sheep-trod now leads us alongside the wall over the moorland ridge of Ramshaw, eventually descending the steep end to a wall-corner. After negotiating the stile here go down with the original wall to by-pass Carleton Biggin by means of stile and gate to emerge onto the farm road.

Turn left down the track and with the lane ahead in sight, locate a stile in the accompanying wall and cross the field to a similar stile. From it descend to the sprawl of barns at Carla Beck Farm, using a step-stile midway along a fence: pass between the buildings directly behind it to debouch via a stile onto a lane. Turn left to re-enter the village, varying the finish by squeezing between the first houses on the right, emerging by the church.

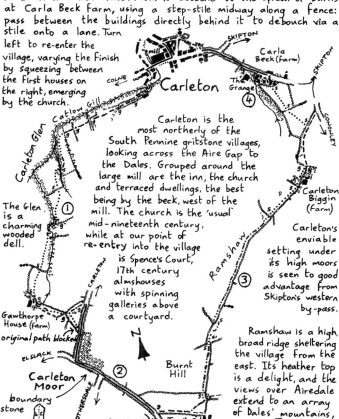

Carleton is the most northerly of the South Pennine gritstone villages, looking across the Aire Gap to the Dales. Grouped around the large mill are the inn, the church and terraced dwellings, the best being by the beck, west of the mill. The church is the 'usual' mid-nineteenth century, while at our point of re-entry into the village is Spence's Court, 17th century almshouses with spinning galleries above a courtyard.

The Glen is a charming wooded dell.

Gawthorpe House (Farm)
original path blocked
EL SLACK
Carleton Moor
boundary stone

Carleton Biggin (Farm)

Carleton's enviable setting under its high moors is seen to good advantage from Skipton's western by-pass.

Ramshaw is a high, broad ridge sheltering the village from the east. Its heather top is a delight, and the views over Airedale extend to an array of Dales' mountains, including Ingleborough.

Burnt Hill

GLUSBURN   Tewit Cote

LOG OF THE WALKS

These two pages provide an opportunity to maintain a permanent record of the walks completed

WALK	DATE	TIME Start	Finish	WEATHER	COMMENTS
1					
2					
3					
4					
5					
6					
7					
8					

WALK	DATE	TIME Start	TIME Finish	WEATHER	COMMENTS
9					
10					
11					
12					
13					
14					
15					
16					
17					
18					

KEY TO THE MAP SYMBOLS

Route   ——clear——   sketchy   no path

Route on public road   wall

unenclosed   Fence/hedge

Abbreviations   g = gate

s = stile c = cattle grid   Railway line

Buildings   Church   Cairns   Limestone

summit other   clints

Crags   Loose rock   Marsh   Trees

/scree

river or beck   reservoir

bridge   waterfall

Miles from start   Direction   N

③   of North

Scale: approximately 2½ inches = 1 mile

THE COUNTRY CODE

- Respect the life and work of the countryside
- Protect wildlife, plants and trees
- Keep to public paths across farmland
- Safeguard water supplies
- Go carefully on country roads
- Keep dogs under control
- Guard against all risks of fire
- Fasten all gates
- Leave no litter - take it with you
- Make no unnecessary noise
- Leave livestock, crops and machinery alone
- Use gates and stiles to cross fences, hedges and walls